MW01167516

The Return of the Fertilizer King

and

Other Tales

by

Mark U. Sturges

Robert D. Reed Publishers • Bandon, OR

Robert D. Reed Publishers
P.O. Box 1992
Bandon, OR 97411
Phone: 541-347-9882 • Fax: -9883
E-mail: 4bobreed@msn.com
web site: www.rdrpublishers.com

Typesetter: **Barbara Kruger**
Cover Designer: **Grant Prescott**
Cover Photo: **Lindsay Cornelius**
Chili Nervanos Farm sign woodcarving by **Wally Eubanks**

ISBN 1-931741-55-7
Library of Congress Control Number 2005900934

Manufactured, typeset and printed in the United States of America

Poems in this book have previously appeared in **Farming Magazine.**

The Red Wheelbarrow was used by the generous permission of New Directions Press.

Shit Shoveler's Retort was used by the gracious permission of Paul Tipton.

Just a time burglar
Stealing through Eternity

M.U.S

This book is dedicated to my father,
William Coyle Sturges,
the original Fertilizer King

Acknowledgments

I want to thank Elaine Ingham for always asking when this book was going to happen. There couldn't have been so many beetles on so many pages if Patricia Q and Dick Richardson, as well as one of the best beetle keysters in the country, Peg, hadn't identified everything I sent to them at the University of Texas at Austin. I think that was the longest sentence I ever wrote in my life. Andy Moldenke was the first entomologist to make me aware of the rare beetles I had living at Chili Nervanos. Thank you Ed Maletis for letting me be me. And my friends at Columbia for letting me just do my job. If it wasn't for my iMac Guru, Terrence Dodge, I'd probably be back to using a Smith Corona Presidential by now. Pat and Sue Reed make the best labels and cards any entramanure ever got to send on a box. Randy Thomas makes the best manure compost tea in the land. He is a Fertilizer King in the truest sense of the term. No one has given me more or better criticism of my writing than Robert McDowell, fellow poet and publisher of Story Line Press. Perhaps there wasn't anyone more instrumental in this than Jane Clark, thank you. After thirty-five years of writing, I didn't really think that Publishers made house calls. Thank you Robert Reed for setting me straight on that one.

Maryanne, thank you so much for all the proofreading and just for putting up with me for all this time. I love you. Everyone knows that Fertilizer Kings are not the best housekeepers.

Contents

The Return of the Fertilizer King

Harry swore   he would never
shop there again,   but   the mystery
of the place   always   pulled him back,
gourmet food and exotic plants. Many times
trouble came from the plants,   but   this was
new.
Now the food
stepped up   Causing the misery   usually
associated with the plants.
It was only last week
when a Wandering Jew
Whispered a racist   pork recipe   to a
Lebanese man looking at lentils.   This man
first glared at Harry.
Then told him he was Muslim.
As he stomped off   he would never
believe that it
was the plant
telling him the recipe.
On his way out   Harry could see him
telling the woman   at the front counter   What
Harry   had said   About the Pork.
Sometimes   even plants could be racists. It was
supposed to be peaceful here.
The Bares Breech Store,
sat   at the dead end   of a side street   called
Ulong,

the only   unpaved   street in town.
Chuck holes everywhere,   gravel   had been extinct
for years   in the Ulong neighborhood. No one
had ever told these people   about location.
Create a place   strange enough   and people will come.
It didn't hurt   that   the place was run
by a tribe of goddesses.
After all these years,
Harry Kingsley   was still a sucker
for a pretty face.
     The young woman who had helped him
was a strawberry blonde named Iris,
with eyes   the color of wisteria.
She was probably twenty-five,
freckles were still   on her nose.
He explained to her
the lamb dish   that would be dinner. The freckles
jumped upon the mentioning   of the lamb.
An invisible shrug   went through his body
as she told him   she was a vegan.
It was then   she had told him   of the big
sale on the marinated   artichoke hearts.
There was   a big indigo spider tattoo
just above her left breast,
at least   it looked like a spider.
It disappeared   into her shirt   just   when he was sure
his identification was correct.

"Was that a spider?" Harry asked.

Smiling,   she pulled down her blouse
to reveal the tattoo
covering her whole left breast.
Somewhere above her nipple
it turned   into a fluttering moth
with baby blue eyes   on the wings.   For a second
he forgot   about the artichokes.

"You don't know now,   do you?"   she giggled.

"Don't know what?" Harry asked.

"Whether it's a moth,   or a butterfly,
or a spider?"

"I thought girls were afraid of spiders."

"Are you?"

"Only black widows   and brown recluses.   I
don't even know what a brown recluse looks like.
So I guess I'm not too scared."

Her blouse was back up.   There was only
the spider.
No moth.   No butterfly.
He wasn't at the nursery   anymore.
He was absentmindedly
cooking his dinner.
Was someone   supposed to come over
He couldn't remember.   There were four lamb
chops.

Two wine glasses.   Too many chops   for
him to eat.
Two glasses   a good clue. Shitakes in the pan,
a big splash   of sauvignon blanc
for deglazing   and now
for the artichoke hearts.
The lid's pretty tight   but   starting to loosen.
One, two, three, four, of the little   six ounce
jars   opened. He'd been so hungry.
The guest hadn't shown.   God Damnit   God
Damnit   Harry was running   Grabbing
Swearing again and again   Here   there
everywhere. The kitchen   had become an
asylum.
The artichokes   had turned
into large, large   indigo colored spiders
running down
the counter tops,
Jumping   into the bowl   of his Kitchen Aid,
another   jumped onto the toaster
and jumped again
on top   of a bottle of olive oil.
They seemed   to be laughing at him.
Harry wondered
if he could get his money back.
He thought of her hair.
He thought of her breasts.
How was he going
to catch these spiders.

Look at the one
on the trapeze web
swinging off of the cupboard.
At least he wasn't afflicted
with arachnophobia.

   He felt better   the next day.
The sun was shining   the birds were singing.
Asiatic lilies were blooming,
the ones   with the creamy white petals
and cinnamon spots.
   Thinking   about the night before
he could still visualize
the spiders   jumping
out of the jars.
He always wished   he had a witness
for events such
as the artichoke spiders,
but sometimes ya just   had to tell people
what went on.
Sometimes   ya had to keep your mouth
shut
This wasn't one of them.
He wanted his money back.
As strange   as the Bares Breech was,
they should   accept his version.
Maybe they could give him a credit   for
something else.

Perhaps he could buy
some kind of a plant   he didn't have.
He didn't want any more   of their bizarre acting
food.

The kitalpa trees
were leafed out,   just starting to bloom.
They reminded him   of the tree
in his grandparents' yard.
He and his brother
had used the seed pods   for sword fighting
in the fall.
His brother
was in prison now.
Harry lived in another town
in another state.
He wondered
if kids   still used the kitalpa pods   for swords.
Nostalgically   he walked down the sidewalk.
He watched   as some sparrows searched
for bugs   in the radiator   of an old
green Cadillac.
The nostalgia   wasn't surprising
considering his grandfather
had been dead   for forty years.
Childhood gone   but still a memory
as he walked   down the street.

    Fortunately
there weren't   any other customers
in the Bares Breech.

The woman   behind the counter
was someone   he'd never seen before.
She smiled at him
as he walked through the door.
Her smile comforted him.
He reached   for his receipt   as he walked
toward her.
    "Good morning," he said confidently.
    "Good morning yourself," she answered.
    He blushed   as he looked
at her hair.
He was sure
she was a raspberry blonde.
Twenty years ago
there wouldn't have been
such a hair color,   but now
anything was possible.
    "What color is your hair?" he asked.
    "I'm probably,   what you would call,
a raspberry blonde."
    "I guessed that, but really didn't believe it."
    "Is there something   the matter with my
hair?"
    "No,   it's great."
    "Are you a beautician?"
    "No, I'm just a guy   returning some artichoke
hearts
I bought here yesterday."
    "Funny, I worked yesterday
but I don't remember you."

"I didn't buy them from you," he said.

"Oh,   who was it then?"

"She had a big blue   spider tattoo," exclaimed Harry.

"Oh, really?   And where   was this tattoo?"

"Right above   her left breast."

"What else did she look like?"

"She had   wisteria colored eyes.   She had freckles on her nose."

"You seem to know her   quite well."

"Never saw her before but   she was pretty funny."

"You're putting me on. I bet you weren't even here yesterday," she said.

"No, I was.   There was much more than the spider. Her breasts   were covered   with a moth or a butterfly   that had blue eyes."

"And she showed you this?"

"Yeah,   she said she was a vegan."

"Half the people who work here   are vegans. What's wrong with the artichokes?"

"I had a bad experience with them last night."

"Oh, I'm so sorry."

"My lamb dish   was almost done. The sauce was reduced perfectly, just where I wanted it. The shitakes were tender," he lamented.

"You yuppies   have it so tough. I may go home
and color my hair green
with envy.
Are you reciting
from a Martha Stewart Cookbook?"

"No,   I'm just trying   to give you the picture   of what actually happened."

"Please continue.   I thought   I was in the audience
of the Chef's   fastest   cooking contest
for a second."

"The aromas
were layering
the kitchen's atmosphere," Harry interjected.

"Do you talk   wine speak too?" she
interrupted again.
"I bet Danielle Steele   is your sister," she
jabbed.

Ignoring her, he continued.

"A harvest moon rose slowly
over the tree line,   filling   the living room
window.
I took   the first lid   off the artichokes
and   the culinary terrorism began.
I don't know   if I'll ever   be the same
cook
I was.   As the lid came off,
the artichoke hearts   turned into very large

spiders and   dashed around the kitchen. The
more jars I opened
the more spiders.   It was   the Kentucky
Derby
on my cutting boards.
I turned off the lamb and
started catching   the biggest arachnids I had
ever seen
outside of *Arachnophobia*.   These babies were
huge.   I wondered if their brothers and sisters
were movie stars. As I caught them   and put
them   back into their jars,
they turned   back into artichoke hearts."
    "Julia Child   and the yuppies
have really changed cooking   the last few
years,
but even Julia   never had this happen to her."
    "Just think
how horrible
it would have been
if I was afraid of spiders," he said.
    "You know   what the weirdest thing
about this is; what's your name   by the way?"
    "Harry Kingsley."
    "The weirdest thing   about this, Harry,
is that   I half believe you."
    "Lunacy may be in vogue,   but   it's not
something
I'm into."
    "Did that girl   that sold you   the artichokes
have purplish-blue eyes?"

"Yeah,　　they were wisteria colored."

"Iris Langley,　　the daughter　　of the owner.
She's a witch.　　She hasn't been around
for a long time.

Nothing is ever the same
when she's in town.
I can't believe
I didn't see her yesterday."

"I don't think　I have ever seen the owner.
What's her name?" asked Harry.

"Wisteria Langley. She's　　not around much either.
She always shows up
in late spring　gone before the middle of June."

"Is she here now?"

"No, but　she said　she would be back
this afternoon."

"Would you like to open　　one of these jars
just to see　what happens?"

"It wouldn't do any good.
Iris' sense of humor　would cast
a one-time spell to make you look silly
if you were trying　　to convince someone
of your story."

"So yer saying that they're probably okay
now?"

"Did you open all of them?"

"Yeah."

"We could open every one of these　　and
they would just be　　artichokes."

"What's your name?"

"Daphne Lane."

His eyes   circled the room
seeing the place for the first time,
though   he had been here   many times.
Old scales   cobwebs clinging
to their faces,
Packages of seeds,
their names
faded   on a shelf just   out of reach.
    "Does anyone   buy stuff   off of   those
high shelves?"
    "Not often."
    "Aren't   those seeds   too old to
germinate?"
    "I don't know; Wisteria said
they were antiquity.
Someday,   someone   would want them.
She said   someone   would have the soil
to bring Lazarus
back from the dead.
    Those seeds
have been waiting   for him
to walk   through the door."
    A cold chill   ran down his back
as his eyes   spotted an
old canvas bag
even higher   on the wall.
So many times   he had looked
around this store   and
never saw it,
The Spirit of Geronimo Fertilizer Company.

He blinked his eyes and
he was back
twenty-five years.
    His eyes were open.
He was in Bisbee, Arizona,
Chicken coops and chicken shit.
Back   when he had an idea
of what he might do.
The glory   of something   began too early.
He barely remembered
the label   they had created   so long ago,
The old warrior
looking out
from his painted pony.
A four-tined pitchfork
drawn in a circle
on the horse's flanks.
    The label
almost looked new
as he stared at it
through time
from twenty-five feet away.
    "Is that bag   of fertilizer   up on the wall
for sale?"
    "No, it isn't.
You   are the first person
that ever asked about it.
I've never seen anyone
go into a trance
having seen a bag   of fertilizer.

You haven't said anything   for five minutes
since   you first saw it.
Wisteria   has made it
very clear
to anyone
who has ever worked here
that bag
is never   to be moved,
let alone sold.
It's something
of a totem to her."

    "I'll keep the artichokes.
Please ask Wisteria
to hang around   this afternoon.
I really want to see her."

    "Bye, Harry."

    Daphne Lane,
he didn't think he liked her at first.
It must have been
her natural defenses   protecting her
from crazy people.   She actually believed him
about the spiders.
She didn't want to,   but   she was resigned to it
after he explained himself.

    Funnier still,   running into Wisteria,
If it was true   that she was around.
It looked as though
time had treated her well businesswise.

Her store
had been around   as long   as he'd been
living here.
It wasn't that big of a town.
Strange   they'd never   run into each other
before this.
The spiders   must have been
part of the plan.
Who really was her daughter?

      He never really thought much
about those old days
In Bisbee and Tombstone.
      He always thought
that old days
were for old people.
So many   of the old people
were gone   and   as much   as he hated to
admit it
he was one   of those people now
though
he didn't feel old.
      An emptiness   surrounded him
for an array   of the people   who were gone.
There were people
who   used to be friends   but   drifted away.
With Wisteria,
he could   never quite reconcile
the difference
between

someone gone   and
someone dead.   If you never saw
either one   of them
what was the difference?
     Sometimes
he thought   more about   old dead friends
or relatives   than he thought   of live ones.
     Wisteria
had been gone   all these years.
     She was the one
who really really wanted to break up
The Spirit of Geronimo Fertilizer Company.
He hadn't   given it much thought   until now,
but   she had been right.
     What they had been doing
back then   wasn't right.
Everyone   except Wisteria
had thought it a great adventure,
Stealing chicken shit for profit.
She had been worried
about going to jail   or someone
getting shot   over doing something   really
stupid.
     It was much more than that.
Even twenty years ago,
they had been rebels   against chemical
fertilizers,
but   they had missed   the really big
picture.

Wisteria   had probably seen it,   but   the
rest of them
were too caught up
in the adrenaline rush.
None of them   had seen the relationship
between the people
who owned the chickens
and the   chicken shit rustlers.   Because
there hadn't been one.
Their thoughts were how
fast they could empty Rhode Island Red's
chicken coops.
of their aviary guano.

Wisteria   was the only
one who had seen   how stupid it was
stealing something
that people   would have given them
if they'd only asked.
Things were clearer
twenty-five years later.

The Red Wheelbarrow

so much depends
upon

a red wheel
barrow

glazed with rain
water

beside the white
chickens.

William Carlos Williams

Shit Shoveler's Retort

Should I see:
One, two, three yearling colts
bobbing heads and flicking ears.
feet tucked under, lying in the paddock
facing the sun, front still grabbbing at the
shadows?

And should I be sarcastic
about the rich smell
and visual texture of horse turds?
Should I avoid feeling the stiffness
of the leftover military boots I wear?

How can I be bitter about the forms
taking shape in the sun
as my breath takes shape:
rimrock extrusions, the angularity of houses,
the goingeverywhereness of black oak branches?

I cannot be what Whitman was –
I want to wear my own hat as I please
And I have only a silver wheelbarrow,
not a striking red one, like Williams.
I can only be what I am, today.

I can only see the black tomcat on the fence-rail
stalking sparrows in the leafless blackberry vine.
I can only stay a short while here
with tobacco, coffee, and these words –
then I go back to shoveling and spreading shit.

Paul Tipton

Decades and Centuries of Wheelbarrows and Manure

for Bill and Diane Swartz

A flight of twenty meadowlarks
lands among the Alpacas
between the blades of blowing
grasses on a ridge
in the coast range
on top of the Pacific.
Somewhere a crow calls
a ratchet stuck in his throat.
The pile of Alpaca manure
smaller than last week
Members of the herd
moving to other parts
of the country   after their sale.
They say Animals cost less
on the West Coast.
The road is muddy
Fear of getting stuck
keeps one further   from the pile
The pitchfork only stretches so far.
Orchard grass and Alpaca pellets.
One fork full   another another
Sticks to the boots
Stains the pants
Overalls   Overalls, One fork full, then another

Six goats, take audience on the fence
One, two, three, rub their faces
on the voltless electric wire.
One scratches, a stubby little horn.
One fork full   Another.

In another pasture
just across the road
Six Alpacas, watch for a while.
Then,   with their guardian llama
Astro travel   to the Andes
joining with their
Brothern and Sistern

The Rain turns   Left
into a sunny sky and
the Pacific goes flat
Gray Whales   migrate   down below
But up here, it's just, one fork full
after another   cloud bank passes
off to the north.

Occasionally the alpaca berries
are too dry,   they fall through the tines
these berries would not adorn
a bowl of cornflakes
never be   never be
the star of a cheese cake.

Five or six months
this poop is soil again.
But Now   it's just one fork full

sometimes a shovel
Much as Tipton
With his silver wheelbarrow
Maybe William Carlos Williams
with his red one.
At Chili Nervanos
waiting for this shipment
the big orange one   too heavy to lift empty
heavier yet   filled with Alpaca droppings.
Perhaps, these garbage cans
full of dung   will fill the   state of the
art   gray
plastic wheelbarrow   which arrived for
Christmas.

   The Alpacas   are
back at the fence
Having returned   from Chile.
A rusty one
A white one
Walking sweaters   Looking   Looking
Back to the Andes
Wheelbarrows   and   Manure
Williams in New Jersey
Tipton in Rusch, Oregon
Sturges in Gold Beach, Oregon
High on the Ridge Line
Shovelling shit
in a new century
Still looks   Still Smells
The Same.

Up at Mel Luckie's Place

for Mel

It's November
in the Pumpkin Patch
The Sun still shines
The kids are gone
Home   or at school
Halloween is over   but
its threats
of tooth decay   linger
Halloween's
Not a night
for diabetics

                              A night for
                              Saints and Souls
                              good and bad
                              wishing
                              for a return
                              to the walking plain
                              to the airways
                              to the waterways
                              dark of night Adventurers
                              waiting   waiting
                              seeking power
                              from here to D.C.

The spooky graveyard
stands   on the hill

amongst the six foot   seedling firs
the maze   of skeletons   hides silently
in the stand   of pines
Music   of the Grateful Dead
                    Stored
                    for another season

Pumpkins are still everywhere
the ground is orange
the packing shed
houses   straw bales   straw bales
more pumpkins
big ones   little ones   in-between ones
gourds   carpet the floor
corn stalks
tied to the beams
of Headquarters

can't get any dryer

Two Scare Crows
sit silently
at a Picnic Table
four feet away
The green John Deere
baseball cap
faces North   held in place
by a safety pin
on the burlap head
the bill   shading
the table   not his   black button eyes
                 not his   material stuffed cranium

nor the face
Looking south
At least the guy
is still sitting up.

His buddy is
collapsed next
to him   on the bench
Maybe it's a her
She's kind   of a heap.
A melt down
of cloth   straw   burlap
Overalls in pretty   good shape
one burlap arm
coming out   of a faded
flannel shirt
nicely sewn into
a nice quality   of gunny sack.   But
the black hat   covering
her fabric face
doesn't reach   the table level.

Four Hundred Pumpkins
didn't go home
to a front porch
Four hundred pumpkins
never became a face
Now   they wait to rot
Now   they wait to   become worm food
Now   they wait to   become worm
     composition

are they writing letters
are they still Pumpkins
Or are they
now worms   going
to Idaho
Maybe Montana
wonder   if they are
the compost   going to New Jersey   Next spring

Decay   is all around us.
One day a
Jack O Lantern
The next day
Worm shit
What about   the Pie   for Thanksgiving?

The wind is Still
The Leaves are
doing   a slow turn
The Sun   is a warm friend
sitting lightly
on the backs
of flannelled shoulders   And
Once again
Mr. Luckie's place
is a Christmas Tree Farm.

The King Is Gone

Sometimes it rained hard
sometimes   it didn't rain   at all
Then it got cold, then it hailed.
They showed up
after a particularly
vicious windstorm.
That's when they
always appeared.
Dave the druggist
raised pheasants
for him and his labradors.
Once after near
hurricane winds
Ninety escaped when
their house blew over.
The weeks following
that blow found
the Chinese descendants
at large
in cranberry bogs
in the woods   driveways
dogfood dishes
everywhere   food might be handy.
A rooster and three hens
took a great liking
to our wooded driveway.

After a while
they were gone.
Too many raccoons
Too many skunks
Too many neighbors' cats
Had they really
sneaked up the driveway?

Two years later
a sudden gust
an open door
The King   of Rosa Road
was back
Every day visible
standing in front
of an abandoned
piecemeal Subaru station wagon
hidden in a hedge.
The old car
with a blue tail-gate
and brown sides
was the Rock of Gibraltar
the Monarch
stood in front
of   day after day.
Standing so straight
Made one think
of George Washington   crossing the Delaware.

His rednecked uniform
was so bright
standing there in front
of that abdicated vehicle
Hail   falling   around his face
Always in that same spot.
The car   is still there
It has no license
An old purple   Station Wagon
Registered to no one
claimed only
by a hole
in the hedge. But once again
The King is Gone.
Long Live the King.

Drumming

for Clint Josey

The sound
        first appeared
        in spring   coming
                out of the woods
                in one direction
                then another
                soft always soft

        A blue jay screeched
        A warbler warbled
        Distractions
        only small distractions

        The sound travelled
        beyond the woods
        it stayed in your
        head a hundred miles
away.
        Two weeks later
        it came back
        July
                August

                        September.
                        Was it the same
                        drum or was

it a pileated woodpecker
pounding a hole
in a dead alder.
                    Was it a pileated
                    woodpecker pounding
fifty holes
in a dead alder
waiting for those
holes to change
into   the carpenter ant Hotel.
Waiting   for the Pileated Pub
to serve   Autumn alder dust
covered ants.

was that the
drumming

or was it a decade
ago on Aitu Taki
a wedding ceremony
announcement
circling   the seven mile   Island

the Spring drumming
in the woods
was calling   for a wedding
Mr. Grouse was calling
for his fiance.

The drumming
sounding through

the summer rain
brought   all the times
all the miles
and all the seasons
to the same woods
On the same morning.

The Bottle Collector

for Robert McDowell

The Bottle collector
dashed across
two lanes of Southbound Traffic
wearing   a long coat
sometimes worn
by garage mechanics
he scooped
up a dead raccoon
off the double   yellow line
adjacent   to the Mill Casino
In a different place
In a different time
he could have been
a cornerback
for the University   of Oregon
he could have been
the free safety   for Holy Cross
grabbing fumbles
on the grid iron
In the Fall   On Saturday afternoons
but not now
his uniform
is a coverall
without breaking stride
he races

back   across the
same two lanes
a step ahead
of two busses   and a log truck
never losing
the gleam in his eye
he gently lays
the dead raccoon
in amongst his
bottles and cans.

Tuesday

for Paula Baudry

A light southerly
rippled the
post office flag.
The Trundel D
Was a fishing boat
sitting on a funky
trailer a block away
with three other derelicts.
They cried out
for paint
they cried out
for a scraping
they begged
for a sandblaster's nozzle.
The Trundel's wheelhouse
shouted poverty
It chided in
Mariner terms
"You'd be glad   to see me
if you was drowning."
You wouldn't think
I was the ugliest
on the south coast
If you was

foundering
on the bad side
of a twenty-footer."
"You wouldn't care
that my wheelhouse
was perched two feet
from my prow."

Wild fennel
tried to hide
The "Parking for
Sea Breeze Florist"   Sign
No One was
buying any flowers.
Not even a bicycle
out front.

Inside Pitch's Tavern
Men and Women
smoked cigarettes
drank beer
In the men's restroom
a red-headed
nude with perky tits
stood above the
commode wearing
only a small
flower tattoo
on her thigh.
the artist signature

was PAB.
Grafitti was missing
on the walls
Out of respect
to her flesh
and her
nice looking eyes
perhaps some unknown
sailor's superstition
protected her virtue
Not much light
for the drinkers
Not much light
for the smokers
Dark as the
charcoal colored dog
sleeping on the floor.
Who might have
had Irish Setter
Blood
Ten or twenty
generations ago.

A drive around
the block   showed
The Trundel D
to actually be
the Thunderbird
Out of Port Orford.
Missing a few   letters
here and there

Had to be
close up
to See who
she really was.

The Fall Flights

John Lennon
   George Harrison are gone
   The rains fall   sometimes
   so misty   portraying   a false sense
of drying invincibility.
   No Lennon or Harrison   but
the beetles remain hopeful.
Flocks   of migratory Robins
covering the orchard Floor   one afternoon
eerily gone the next.
Flights   of Northern mallards
arriving   in the flooded dairy lands
their bright orange feet
extended as watery
landing gear   hit the ponds
Flocks   of twenty-five
flocks   of fifty green wing teal
strafe the fence tops
riffle the weeds   ignored   by the summer
Guernseys
Four pintail   dabble   on the other side
of a muddy berm
Thirty-five wigeon
whistle   from just past
a cattail thicket   near the willows.
The night sky
gets fuller and fuller

as Northern Storms
drive more birds south   through gray and
windy atmospheres.

On the other side   of the Valley
other flyers are concentrating
low profiled individuals
Predatory Beetles
flying in from everwhere
escaping   flooded fields
fleeing bird's beaks
Zooming   through vent holes   of compost bins
Feeling safe
suddenly becoming
the top   of the food chain.
Running now only
from the light.
Dining Dining Dining
A rove beetle
scurries   through blue kernels
that once sat
in a jar   as white basmati
the skinny wiggly
black beetle
chomping rice weevils.
There's ten more
having a microscopic dinner
on a batch   of discarded potato salad.

A red amphodium dung beetle
desiccates the llama berries

filling the thousand gallon
stainless steel tanks.
The rotten orange carcasses
of two thousand pumpkins
float   on the tons   of manure.
A congress   of beetles
skating across
the orange flows   Directs the food chain
of flyers and crawlers.
With the Beetles
in charge
it's only poop
for so long.

A golden eagle
flying   across the flooded pasture
searched   for a crippled spoonbill.

Three Hister Beetles
found fifty-five
fly larvae hiding
under   a decaying cabbage leaf
dining dining dining.
A longfaced carabid
consumed a four-inch
banana slug
it caught climbing
up the leg
of a dairy tank.
The arthropod was suave
The slug was slime.

It's a hard day's night
maybe   The White Album
After the waters
had receded
Every one flew away.
Some had feathers
Some had black wing covers.

Under the Purple Plum Tree

A Cougar
screamed
         in the middle
         of the night
         just outside
         the bedroom window.
Chills on a hot night
just awake
wondering
for a second
if you were
inside   out
of harm's way
just a second
before remembering
all too clearly
you'd died   a few hours earlier.

You were out
there buried
deeply wrapped
in a favorite blanket
Under a plum tree
where last week
you'd stood on
hind legs to
pick purple   fruit

imitating a deer
though you were
a chocolate lab
what about the
time you woke
us in the middle
of the night

when the garage
was full   of smoke.
What about the
hand signalled retrieve
you made
on that greenhead
across the canal
thirty-feet wide
and twelve feet
deep.
Dirk had exclaimed
"the ten thousand dollar
trained dogs
I've hunted with
couldn't do it
any better."

Sleep
doesn't come back
With the big cat

still in the
brush
and you
with all
the memories
underground.

Back Roads

Coming off Libby Loop
right onto Noah
Past what a
guess would have
called a crack farm
with chickens and dobermans
in the yard
A needless
no tresspassing sign
warning people
away
from the fifty-foot   single wide.
Noah down the hill
turning into Red Dyke
Llamas   with horses   on the hillside.
Wetlands   a creek   just off the road
Some houses
displaying landscaped front yards
Others junkyards
Even another a
floating lumber yard
with beams   sailing a pasture
blue tarps
                the jib
                    the foresail

Pit bulls
                    sitting on dog houses
staying out   of the slop
A red tabby
crouches on a bale
of hay   watching twenty-two mallards
and a green wing teal
swimming toward a gate
barely showing   a top rail
Two other small
flocks were just
off the front porch
of a white house
featuring
a two foot deep
front yard lake.
A Billy goat
is eating wet hay
next to a past its prime
240 Z.
Black Berries are the
succession fence
of choice.
Some reddish cows
wander around
wondering when
The Red Dyke
won't have to hold
so much water.

The ducks could
go to Mexico
And the cows
could just be bovines.
The amphibious life
was just too hard.

Up at Cherry Ridge

for Wally and Heike Marie

Standing with Wally
200 wigeon flew
twenty yards overhead
Heike Marie joined us
as a Swainson buteo
a raptor
dove   down the hill
behind the barn
and out of sight
soon   another bunch
of wigeon
came low   over the house   and
just above the trees
at The Cherry Ridge Farm
"Those hawks   are always scaring
the ducks   off of the pond.
Once a Swainson
ate one   of our dumb ducks
right by that gate."

On the way Home
Three buffalo grazed
in a pasture
just below
Heike and Wally's.

At first
I didn't believe
they were really there.
Around another curve
it was true winter
and flooded fields   were everywhere.

Off to the left
A thousand ducks
suddenly jumped up
so many
so close
their wings   must have tickled
one another.
Just behind them
as big   as a piper cub
flew a bald eagle.
He must have thought
it was still
Duck Season.

A Day in Chablis

for Robert, Philippe, and Veronique Drouhin

Seems a long time ago now
We took trains and planes
drove the French Freeways
at a hundred and twenty clicks
and finally   we were at the
end of nowhere
The Chablisians claim
they are more obscure
than the people
in the middle of nowhere.

Hardly anyone comes here
they used to claim.
No one drinks
our wine.
Our young men leave
The windows
in town are broken
Who will be around
to fix them?
The frosts
always set us back
the rot
in September
such a killer.

They want Bordeaux
they want Burgundy
A great wine
tradition was   in big trouble
The growers
were broke
Everyone was demoralized.

Then
along came Robert Drouhin
He changed all that
When he bought vineyards
here thirty years ago.

The Serein
a small river
runs through
this old stone town.
At one end
the water runs through
an old estate
where the old grist mill
stood for time immemorial.
The Serien   is the lifeline.
There's a restaurant
bridging it
at the other end of the village

The food
the wine
the eight different cheeses

sweep me back   to the table
Sweep me back
to the vineyards
with the most famous
name in wine.

Picturesque was a sad
cliche remembering
what the view
above Chablis presented.

The view notwithstanding
everything wasn't perfect.
Row after row after row
were manicured
The limestone rocks
in the soil
were resplendent
    not a cane
not a leaf
out of place.
One could have
eaten off the ground.   But
one might not
have found the grapes so tasty.
    It was one of those
really rainy Septembers
One of those
Rainy Septembers
when the Old Chablisians
wanted to kill themselves.

They wondered   if the rain
would ever stop.
Rot was king
in these manicured rows.

Row after row
cluster after cluster
this was a study
of cause and effect
of cold rain
in late August
and early September
and of what
Better living through
chemistry   could not prevent.
More rows
More rot.
Then the manicure ended
though the vineyards continued.
One row
neat as a pin
The next filled
with a cover crop
Walking suddenly wasn't   as easy
Plants that weren't vines
up to our knees
There were red beetles everywhere
Jean Paul didn't know
what kind they were.
They could be seen
running up and down

the plants between the rows
Everywhere
these red beetles
could be seen flying
as we trudged down the hill
in the Les Clos Vineyard.
Funny thing about
Philippe Drouhin's rows
with his beetles and cover crops
where he didn't allow
any chemicals.
There wasn't any rot.
The grapes were pristine.
Should we say it again?
There wasn't a speck of rot.
Since 1990 Philippe
has had his vineyards organic.
Since 1998
his vineyards   have been Bio Dynamic.
Pretty soon we passed
through the Drouhin rows
and were back in the next Manicure.
Rot and more rot
and more rot.
Give me the red beetles
Give me the Drouhin Chablis.
The end of nowhere
isn't so far away.

September 10, 2002
Chablis, France

Letters to an Amish Minister

from

A Backsliding Buddhist

The Eavesdroppers

Dear David and Elsie

I could hear
the geese
flying south   in the night

I asked Maryanne
if she could hear them

We weren't an
audience   to the sound   of their wingbeats.
We were eavesdroppers
Listening   to their conversations
as they flew   over our woods
on the south Coast
Maybe
going hundreds   of miles
to Richvale
Maybe   they were just
going to Langlois.

Sometimes
the rain pounded
Other times
it just dripped
Yet
on five different occasions

one could hear
the flyers   discussing events
as they flew
the Red Eye
To Northern California
In a turbulent night sky.

The language   seemed the same
from all the flocks.
Maybe
they were Snow Geese
Maybe
Little cities
in the air
of Cacklers
Too Early
for   Duskies
        Too High pitched
for Honkers.

Only guesses   could be made
for it was too dark.
Moonless
with little visibility
outside   the bedroom window.

They may have
been voicing concerns
over the recent
opening
of waterfowl season

Maybe that's why
they were flying
under the cover   of darkness.

I don't think
they were discussing
war or peace.

Probably centered
more on organics
and the rice crop
they would see
and taste
once they arrived
at the Lundbergs   in Richvale
Tomorrow.

Forests and Kitchen

Dear David and Elsie

Heathers in the orchard
shafts of light
filtering   through the connifers
Bathing the deathcaps
(phalloides) if one is looking
for Latin
Huckleberries
still sticking   to their bushes
gone in a week or two
Down the crops
of flocks   of migrating robins.

In the Humus
Chantrelles   are still sprouting
The intermittent rain
The intermittment sunshine
keeping the microclimate
in perfect condition
for the mushrooms'
continued fall appearances
and extraordinary sizes.
This one so big
it barely fits
in the pail
as the corkscrew knife

slices through its stem.
This specimen dwarfs
the other orange golden
fungus resting
in the bottom   of the bucket.

Now it's dark
tromping through the
salal and blackberries
thinking about eating
this giant   for dinner

This mushroom
is a little soggy
yet still beautiful.
A whole different
world happening
under examination
in the kitchen.

Wonder what kind
of mites these are
running every which way?
Most of them can
be wiped off
with a wet towel.

What do vegetarians
do at times like these?

I know some
carnivores don't worry much
Though I hate giving
away secrets
but
Nadine Gordimer
says you must
write as if you'd
been dead twenty-five years

But back   to dinner.
Preparations
were under way
for a chicken thigh
extravaganza   featuring big strips
of chantrelles   floating alongside   kalamata
olives
in a chardonnay   dijon mustard sauce.

That was
the objective   as I began
to lightly sear   the mushroom
in the Vignalta Olive oil.

The cast iron pan
had barely begun
to heat up
when a member
of forest floor community
began to emerge   from a crack
in one   of the large   pieces of chantrelle.

This was experiencing
Naturalism at its
finest.
A delay of dinner
was mandated
while I gently removed
the tiny forest visitor
using the tip
of a Wusthoff
Paring knife.
Putting the knife
on the counter
I watched him
jump off the blade.
He couldn't have
had any bad burns
He was still   moving pretty well.

What a dinner side track
this was turning into.
I'd never really
been in the presence
of a pseudo scorpion.   Seen them in pictures
but   never in my dinner.

Running to my office
I grabbed a slide
and cover slip.
Getting back

before he escaped
I used the cover
slip to slide him
onto the slide
and added a drop
of water to hold
the cover slip in place.

Back in my office
I turned on my microscope
and found that
I'd put his
dark purple hairiness
upside down   on the slide.
His pinchers and tail
were moving sideways
and backwards.
I thought it would
be okay to turn
the slide upside down
as the cover slip
was stuck to the slide   by the drop   of
water.
Turning the slide over
the slip cover
and my wee scorpion
fell into the microscope.
Not to be seen again.
Sometimes a Chef
Sometimes a Scientist
The chicken   was Excellent.

Patience

Dear David and Elsie

In the dog days
of summer
I sometimes   lament the thought
of fresh tomatoes
disappearing   from the garden
already thinking   of what its
appearance   would be
once the summer heat   was gone.
Pictures of faded flowers
brought an end   of season melancholy.
Wandering thoughts
vanishing   with the last
of the lemon cucumbers

Thoughts   of sounds
as easy   as the leaves falling
away from the trees
Sounds as frenetic
as the fairchild squirrels
yelling from fir to fir
or the cones
falling and bouncing
off the wooden bins
sometimes even the feeling
of a squirrel chewed

fir cone bouncing
off the Dorfman Pacific Hat
riding on my head.
Luckily for me
the cones aren't   any larger
than three or four inches.
Fantasies   of pinion pine cones
could be unconsciousness.

Summer's exit
shouldn't be lamentable.
What's sad about
Late apple varieties
trying to break
Limbs off the Melrose
Limbs off the Arkansas black
How much cider
is still hanging
from that loaded   Ida Red tree?

Fall is a patient time.
Look at the fig tree
out the bedroom window
Its first seven years
not yielding one fig.
Called a Neverella
We wondered if

it would ever
give us anything.
It still makes us wait.
Someone once said
that maybe Neverella
meant never.   But
the wait
has paid off.
The middle   of October   it starts doling
out its work
of the last year.
its figs are medium size
for months
then the last four   or five days   they
double in size   and begin to turn gray.
A little darker
than the Armadillo Crustace (sow bugs)
that flock to each fig
as it gets riper   and riper.

Fall   is the reward   of patience
Shining   an aspen glow
off the hard shells
of unfrosted pumpkins
waiting for a
late November fig
and Neverella
Doesn't mean Never.

We Must Be Rich

Dear David and Elsie

      Was there ever
a naturalist   who proclaimed
"One could always
tell the wealth
of a man
by the size
of his pumpkin pile
in late November?"
As the pile grew
so did the
populations   of other
foresty inhabitants
Raccoons were pretty
obvious by their
seed stealing holes
punched   in the soft spots
They only seem
interested in the   big white seeds
Composting pumpkin pie
appeared to not
be their forte.

The real connoisseurs
of the big gold squash
are a six legged

black animal
called   an Argytid Beetle
The King and Queen
of the Fall to Winter   Cycle.
Not much is
seen or written
about these animals.
A natural history
Pamphlet   out of California
reports   them being seen
in only five states.
Kentucky, California

obviously Oregon,
maybe Washington
I don't know
the other one.
The reference
says they show up
When the weather   turns nasty
Two weeks into
October   we had two days
of cold rains
Magic   there they were
The first scouts
were in the   compost bins.
Swallows to Capistrano
Argytid Beetles
Showing up at   Chili Nervanos.

Last year
they decomposed
One and a half tons
of pumpkins in
two and a half months.
The Argytids look
over the pumpkin supply
and then   they breed their way
into proper numbers
to accomplish the job.

If one were
a beetle voyeur
the good life
would be at hand.
Less than a month
after seeing the
first adults
larvae are wiggling
everywhere
Pumpkins are becoming

the richest of soil.
Almost before
one's eyes
Tired   Jack O Lanterns
Become the   Bordellos and Nurseries
of these great
soil makers.

It rains
the winds blow
it gets colder   and colder
The Argytids   stay around
producing compost
and more compost
until April comes
One day   they aren't there anymore.
Where did they go?
Where did they come from?

Calls start coming in
from all over the country
"We need that
scarab compost"
They really don't
say that
Everyone thinks the
earthworms do it all   but
the big Pumpkin
pile says it
just isn't true.
In January
this heap will
be wiggling with
beetle larvae.
It's November
our pile is huge
We must be rich.